Philippians

Pursue Christ's Joy

Sarah K. Howley

Flaming Dove Press

Flaming Dove Press
an imprint of
InspiritEncourage LLC
1520 Belle View Blvd #5081
Alexandria, VA 22307
www.inspiritencourage.com

ISBN 978-1-960793-30-0 (e-pub)
ISBN 978-1-960793-31-7 (paperback)
ISBN 978-1-960793-32-4 (large print)

Printed in the United States of America

Contents

Welcome

to this Study of Philippians

Paul wrote this letter the believers in Philippi, a Roman
colony located in Macedonia, or present-day Greece. Most
scholars believe that Paul established this church on his second
missionary journey and that it was the first church in Europe.
Historians think that the city was10-15,000 people in size and
near a trading port. As a Roman colony with Greek heritage, the
city hosted a multitude of languages and worship practices.

Scholars believe that Paul wrote this letter from prison, either
while in Ephesus or in Rome. The letter addressed the fledgling
church in Philippi about a number of topics but perhaps
had the primary intention of thanking the group for their
generous financial support. The letter included calls to unity and
harmony as well as warning about false teachers and teachings
and guidance on ways to serve others.

This short letter is hard to overlook, as it includes a number of
often quoted verses of encouragement so many believers rely on
daily. The epistle is frequently cited for the multiple references
to joy, but Paul included numerous strong exhortations on
Christian life. This study sets out to highlight the consistency

of God's message of encouragement and joy in life through the depth of Paul's words and instruction for Christians today.

Each session opens with warm-up introductory questions, goes on to a reading from Philippians and questions related to the passage. Then the study goes to the linked Old Testament passages and questions. Each study session ends with considerations for personal application. Additional tips and suggestions on approaching the study for individuals and groups follow.

Suggestions for the Study

This study is composed of 5 sessions and is designed for individual or small group study. It is written to encourage thought and discussion of the scripture, encouraging individuals and groups seeking God to have conversations about the biblical text. For 'You will seek me and find me when you seek me with all your heart,' as Jeremiah 29:13 says.

General Guidelines for Individual Study

1. Open each session with prayer. Ask God to speak through his Word.

2. Respond to the Introduction questions to focus on the theme of the session and what Jesus says in the main reading.

3. Read the passage more than once. Using different translations can offer expanded viewpoints on the meaning of the original text. This study uses the New International Version (NIV) as the basis of questions and quotes. However, any version may be used to provide insight and assist in revealing meaning.

4. This study is designed to offer a starting point for the discovery of what God has to say to you through his Word. Because the study looks at how the Old Testament is reflected in the epistles, there are observation and interpretation questions about the readings in Ephesians and then about the links in the Old Testament, as well as comparisons between the passages. These are followed by application questions for personal and group discussion. Writing your responses will provide clarity and focus your thoughts on the verses.

5. Use a Bible dictionary or other reference books to look up any unfamiliar words, places, or names.

General Guidelines for Group Study

1. Come to sessions prepared. Some groups will choose to read and respond ahead of time then gather and discuss together; others will gather to read and discuss together. Before beginning, agree how the group would like to proceed so everyone is prepared.

2. Be an active participant in the group by sharing your thoughts and responses to the questions. Groups often have members who are of varied maturity in Christ and each perspective should be valued.

3. Listen to each other. Consider the amount of time that is available for everyone to share and be careful not to dominate the conversation.

4. Be open. As there are various 'right' answers, be open to considering alternate viewpoints and agree to disagree.

5. Maintain confidentiality of the group. For participants to be willing to share and grow, the trust level in the group must be high. Do not share what anyone says in the group with someone outside the group unless permission is given to do so.

6. Expect God to meet you in the study. His Word is living and active (Heb. 4:12) and he is present when we gather in his name (Matt. 18:20).

Introduction

Paul's story with the believers in Philippi is recounted in Acts 16:11-40. Read this passage and summarize Paul's activities in the town. Then consider how the people in the town viewed him as he engaged in those various activities.

The epistle to the Philippians is often described as having a focus on joy. How do you define *joy*? How do you express joy?

Session 1: Thanksgiving in Suffering

Philippians 1:1-26

Opening

In what situations do you find it easy to thank God? In what situations is it more difficult?

This letter was written by Paul from prison. Many were ashamed to be associated with someone who was in chains or in custody of the Roman government. How has society's reaction to those in prison changed over time?

As mentioned, this letter was written from prison, yet Paul focused on joy despite being confined and socially outcast because of his chains. Instead, Paul embraced the situation he was in and found joy through others and in sharing the gospel. That was just the start of modelling the life of Christ through our actions and attitudes that continued throughout the letter. Remember Paul's situation while continuing the study and ponder his reactions as demonstrated through the letter to this congregation.

Read Philippians 1:1-26.

Reading Questions

What brought joy to Paul according to his opening thanksgiving?

What did Paul say were the benefits of abounding in love?

What was the result of Paul's imprisonment?

What motivations did people have to preach during Paul's time in prison?

What did Paul expect the outcome of his prison time would be?

Summarize Paul's contrasts of the benefits of living and dying.

Old Testament Links

In Philippians 1:12-14, Paul described how suffering brought glory and honor to God. This was a concept which was prevalent in the Old Testament. From Genesis through the Prophets, God's glory came in part from his people's suffering not just in the happy times.

Read about the difficulty that Abraham faced in Genesis 15:1-6,16:1-6, 18:1-15 and 21:1-7. How did he suffer? How was God honored through his suffering?

Though Joseph's story is a long one, consider Genesis 45:3-7 as a summary. What suffering did he undergo? How was God glorified through that suffering?

Application

Consider your own life and the suffering you have endured. How has that brought glory and honor to God?

How have you experienced joy through those circumstances?

Session 2: United as One

Philippians 1:27-2:11

Opening

How would you define *humility*? How would the world define the word?

List two examples of humble people you know.

Paul wrote to the Philippians about how to reflect Christ. He wrote of living worthy of the gospel and of imitating Christ so that they would grow in godliness. He also reminded them that he too was undergoing trials and could identify with their struggles. Together, this encouragement offered an environment where humility could be embraced.

Read Philippians 1:27-2:11.

Reading Questions

What examples did Paul give to "conduct yourselves in a manner worthy," (Philippians 1:27) of the gospel?

What did Paul say would make my joy complete," (Philippians 2:2)?

How would the Philippians be empowered to do what would give Paul such complete joy?

What should be done with selfish ambition?

Summarize the mindset of Christ according to the poem Paul included in Philippians 2: 6-11.

Old Testament Links

It is not clear where the apparent quote came from in Philippians 2:6-11. Some say it is a poem and others a hymn that Paul used because of its message and flow. What is clear, however are the references to Jesus' character from the Old Testament that are found in the quote. In particular there are references from Genesis and Isaiah to consider.

Read Genesis 1:27-28 and Genesis 3:5. What was God's plan for man compared to what man wanted? How did this contrast with Philippians 2:6?

As you read Isaiah 45:22-25 and 53:10-12, look for the language that echoes Paul's poem.

Application

In Philippians 1:27, Paul emphasized working together as one –
in the Spirit and together as one. Consider the work that you
do, whether caring for others, laboring in an office or outdoors,
or volunteering. What techniques or skills are useful in working
with someone? What challenges or distractions make it difficult
for you to "stand firm in one spirit" with others? How can
you apply those techniques or skills to pursue greater unity this
week?

Paul called on the believers in Philippi to follow Christ's example
of humility, taking the very nature of a servant. List other
characteristics of Jesus that are in the poem or implied by it.
Which of these traits are most difficult for you to embrace? How
might you make a small step toward the mindset of humility?

Session 3: Children of God without Fault

Philippians 2:12-30

Opening

The word fear is listed in many dictionaries as being similar to respect, wonder, dread, and reverence. Discuss what "fear of the Lord" means.

List three activities that you do for the Lord. How do you feel about them?

Paul discussed grumbling in our activities and the care of fellow workers in this reading selection. His discussion on grumbling challenges believers to be in such awe of the Lord, that they carry out His will with "fear and trembling". He named two dear workers who assisted him, and indeed even worked in his stead for the Lord. He chose to send these workers to comfort and instruct the Philippians in the Lord. Paul's joy in the Lord extended to how he worked and how he trained others to work in his place. We too have this opportunity to approach God's will and work without grumbling while also sharing the load.

Read Philippians 2:12-30.

Reading Questions

Christ worked our salvation, once and for all time. What then did Paul mean by "work out your salvation"?

How, or by whom, is the "working out" accomplished, according to Philippians 2:13?

What did a believer need to do to "shine like a star"?

Name two characteristics of Timothy according to the passage.

Why was it necessary to send Epaphroditus back to Philippi?

Why had Epaphroditus been sent to Paul?

Old Testament Links

Grumbling in the New Testament often references the frequent complaints of the Israelites as they wandered the wilderness. The striking contrast between the gifts that God gave them and the way that they moaned about the gifts is drawn to the forefront of the picture of how Paul worked in these few verses. Paul's call to work without grumbling is not a new one and yet continues to be a challenge still today.

Exodus 17:1-3, Numbers 16:41, 21:4-5, and Deuteronomy 6:13-19 offer examples of the grumbling of the Israelites. Consider the parallels of the passages with Paul's notes to the Philippians. How was the Israelites attitude toward God and his work described?

Read from the Song of Moses in Deuteronomy 32:5-6,12-18 and read Daniel 12:2-3. Describe the "crooked and warped generation" that Paul mentioned and identify the characteristics that one who shines like the stars should have.

Application

What situations tempt you to complain or argue? What changes might help make them more joyful pursuits?

Paul honored Timothy and Epaphroditus for their service to others. What might you do this week that would emulate their service and bring glory to God?

Session 4: Boast in Christ

Philippians 3:1-4:1

Opening

Who did you look up to as a child? Describe the person's character in detail.

What does it mean to be a citizen of a place? What are the rights and responsibilities?

Paul turned from discussing his fellow workers to the worldly qualifications that he leaned on, and many of us may lean on today to establish prestige. Paul, however, discarded worldly acclaim and prestige, calling them kitchen scraps. Paul called believers in this city to embrace Christ and Christlikeness, as well as seek it in others. This same call remains for believers today.

Read Philippians 3:1-4:1.

Reading Questions

What caused Paul to rejoice?

What characteristics did those who "boast in Christ" have?

What did Paul list as his worldly achievements or advantages? Why did he consider these advantages to be garbage or lost?

What qualities did Paul then choose to take on once those were lost? What did he say the status of those qualities were?

Contrast the enemies of the cross to the citizens of heaven. What was the character of each group, according to Paul?

Old Testament Links

In this passage Paul touched on several points in regard to the identity of the Israelites and God's people. Speaking of circumcision, encountering his Spirit, and knowing God all brought to mind the special relationship God had with the Israelites and applied it to the new relationship with the Philippians. This identity is also made available to us today through the same relationship with Christ.

Read Deuteronomy 10:12-22, 30:6, Jeremiah 31:33, Ezekiel 36:25-30 and describe the circumcision that Paul was referencing. Note the actions of the Spirit as well. Who was responsible for the newness of heart that Paul discussed?

Exodus 6:7 and 33:12-13 describe the context for "knowing" God. One is a statement of contract or decision and the other of relationship. List how each verse illustrates that relationship. How did this vary from how Paul described knowing God?

Application

Just as Paul listed the credentials he previously leaned on; we too can be tempted to lean on our qualifications. Which achievements or "gains" are you tempted to rely on instead of Christ?

The Philippians were reminded that their citizenship is in heaven in Philippians 3:20. How does this perspective help you handle today's priorities and worries? What might change in our daily lives in light of this eternal perspective?

Session 5: Rejoice in the Lord

Philippians 4:2-23

Opening

What kinds of things make people anxious and why? List at least three examples.

How do you define contentment?

This portion of Paul's letter to the Philippians encompassed a number of spiritual practices, including fellowship, rejoicing, prayer, meditation, and caring for others. Though each is only touched on, his exhortations invite deep reflection. These practices help develop Christlikeness in the original readers of Paul's letter and continue to do so today.

Read Philippians 4:2-23.

Reading Questions

What can be understood of the relationship between Euodia and Syntyche in Philippians 4:2-3?

What did Paul say to do with anxiety?

What is the result of prayer according to Paul?

Summarize the kinds of things that Paul instructed believers to think upon.

What did the text say was the secret to contentedness?

How did Paul describe the gift of the Philippians?

Old Testament Links

Paul made only passing references to the Old Testament in this
final selection of Philippians. However, the statement that most
called attention to the Scriptures was a valuable reminder of
relationship with God. This idea of personal relationship with
God ran through the Old as much as the New Testament,
inviting believers into intimacy with God and reminding us of
his promises.

The nearness of the Lord may refer to two distances.
Read Deuteronomy 4:7; Psalm 34:17-18, 119:150-151, and
145:18-20; Joel 1:15; Zephaniah 1:7. What are two kinds of
"nearness" as described in the Old Testament? How do they
both support Paul's exhortations?

Application

Paul mentioned dwelling the mind on what is true, noble, and admirable. What thoughts tend to dominate your mind? How might you take steps to shift your focus?

Paul said he learned the secret of contentment. What is one area of life where you struggle to find such contentment? What might help you move toward contentment?

Conclusion

Throughout the letter, Paul pointed the Philippians toward living for Christ and leaving behind worldly things. He called on believers to imitate others who seek the Lord and focus their minds on Christ.

Based on the teachings in the epistle, how would you summarize Paul's instructions on Christlikeness?

What did you learn about God in this study?

What did you learn about yourself in this study?

Do you believe that Jesus is the Messiah, the Son of God and have you received life in his name? If so, describe the qualities of that life.

If this is the first time that you have answered yes to the call of following Jesus, please reach out to a local church or the author to share of your choice and find support for your new life.

To continue your deep dive into "Seeing the Old Testament in the Epistles", pick up *1&2 Peter* to continue your study. Find it at your nearest retailer by scanning the QR code today.

Buy
1&2
Peter
Today

Also By Sarah K. Howley

Seeing the Old Testament in the Epistles
Ephesians: Experience God's Power
James: Know God's Wisdom
1&2 Thessalonians: Prepare for Christ's Return
Hebrews: Elevate Jesus

The Son Reveals the Father
I Am: An 8-Session Study of John
Heart: A 12-Session Study of Luke
Word: An 11-Session Study of Matthew
King: An 8-Session Study of Mark
Our Trustworthy God: How Much God loves You, Joyfully
Engages with You, and Trusts You

Women of the Old Testament Bible Studies
Hope: A Bible Study of Women in Jesus' Lineage
Faith (coming 2025)
Love (coming 2026)

Alive Again Bible Study on Forgiveness
Alive Again: Find Healing in in Forgiveness
Alive Again Bible Study: Find Healing in Forgiveness
Alive Again Forgiveness Prayer Journal

About the Author

Sarah K. Howley is a Bible teacher, passionate about helping believers grow spiritually and take on the character of Christ. She is the founder of InspiritEncourage, an author, speaker, and trained Christian counselor. She has lived in over five countries on four continents and takes her own espresso wherever she goes. Sarah and her husband support initiatives for feeding the hungry and for expanding access to reading.

You can find Sarah on Facebook and Instagram @inspiritencourage. To book Sarah as a speaker at your next event, please contact her through her website. For weekly encouragement and information on her latest releases, sign up for Sarah's newsletter at InspiritEncourage.com.

InspiritEncourage